Don't Open the Door

By: L. Logan

OCTOBER 3, 2023

Contents

Chapter 1.

The rain pattered against the window as Dean and Kathryn sat on the floor, surrounded by an assortment of board games and puzzle pieces.

"I'm so bored," complained Kathryn. She scanned the room for something more engaging. "Can't we do something else?"

Dean's dark hair fell into his eyes as he glanced at his younger sister. An idea popped into his head, making him grin.

"Hey, why don't we try to play that Roblox game, 'Doors'?" he suggested. "I've heard it's like a mystery adventure where you have to find hidden keys and solve puzzles to get through different rooms."

Kathryn's face lit up. "That's a great idea!"

They scrambled to their computers. The screens flickered to life, displaying the Roblox app. They selected the game "Doors."

"Ready?" Dean asked.

"Ready!" Kathryn replied.

They clicked the "Play" buttons on their computer at the same time.

A sudden gust of wind blew through the room, catching Dean and Kathryn off guard. It whipped their hair around wildly, making them squint against the unexpected breeze.

"Did you leave a window open?" Kathryn yelled over the howling wind.

"Of course not!" Dean shouted back, but before he could say anything else, an ear-splitting crack of thunder shook the house.

"Wow!" Kathryn said, her eyes wide with surprise. "That was close!"

"Too close," muttered Dean, his heart pounding in his chest.

Outside, the storm intensified, and the siblings watched in awe as lightning flashed crazily in the sky, illuminating their darkened room with bright streaks of light. The electric energy seemed to dance around them, the air crackling with power.

"Maybe we should get away from the windows," said Kathryn.

"Good idea," said Dean. But just as they started to move away, a blinding flash filled the room, forcing them to shield their eyes with their arms.

"Ouch!" Kathryn cried out, rubbing her eyes.

"Are you okay?" Dean asked, blinking rapidly to clear his own vision. When he managed to open his eyes, however, he realized that they weren't in their home anymore. They were standing in the ornate lobby of a grand hotel – the very same hotel from the Doors game!

"Umm, Dean?" Kathryn stammered, her voice a mixture of wonder and fear. "Where are we?"

"Looks like we're in the game, Kathryn," Dean said, his mind racing as he tried to understand what just happened. "But how is this possible?"

"Hey, look on the bright side," Kathryn said. "At least we didn't have to download anything!"

"Very funny," Dean rolled his eyes. "But seriously, we need to figure out how to get back home."

"Right," agreed Kathryn, staring at their new surroundings. "But first, we should find a way to avoid that creepy Eyes creature. I don't want to risk getting hurt in here."

She pointed at a group of creepy floating eyes watching them from an opening in the wall.

"Agreed," said Dean. He squinted at the eyes. They blinked and floated like they were waiting for them. "Let's explore the hotel and see if we can find any clues on how to get back home – and avoid those floating eyes while we're at it."

Together, they ventured deeper into

the mysterious world of Doors.

Chapter 2.

The grand lobby of the haunted hotel loomed before Dean and Kathryn, as they stepped cautiously into the vast space. Towering walls adorned with tattered wallpaper stretched upwards, swallowed by darkness, as if the ceiling was hiding from their gaze. The dim glow of flickering chandeliers cast eerie shadows on the floor, dancing like spirits in the night.

"Wow, this place is creepy," Kathryn whispered, her eyes wide as she scanned the room.

"Definitely," Dean agreed, his fingers tightening around an old shake flashlight he found on the floor.

A haunting melody drifted through the air, piano notes that seemed to float from nowhere and everywhere all at once. The music sent a chill down Dean's spine.

"Where's that coming from?" Kathryn asked, her voice barely audible above the melancholic tune.

"Must be the intercom," Dean suggested, trying to locate the source of the music. "It's setting the mood of the game, I

10

guess." He couldn't help but admire the attention to detail in the game's design, even though it made his heart race with unease.

"Great," Kathryn muttered sarcastically. "Just what we need – mood music."

Dean smirked. "Yeah, like in a scary movie."

The once-gleaming brass fixtures had dulled over time, and cobwebs clung to every available surface, giving the entire hotel an air of decay and disuse.

"Look at all these elevators," Kathryn said, her eyes wide as she took in the sight of the various doors, each one beckoning them to explore what lay beyond.

"Which one do you think we should choose?" Dean asked, his gaze flitting from door to door, trying to see any differences between them.

"Wait, there are other people here too," Kathryn whispered, pointing towards small groups of players huddled by different elevator doors. Their body language showed their unease – some were nervously wringing their hands, while others paced back and forth, heads down, deep in thought.

"Maybe we should ask them what they know about the game," Dean suggested, though he couldn't shake off the feeling that perhaps not all of these players could be trusted.

"Or maybe we can just pick a random door and hope for the best," Kathryn said. Dean watched as she closed her eyes and spun around, her finger extended like a spinning compass needle.

"Okay, okay," he said, trying to suppress his laughter. "Let's go with that one." He pointed to a particular elevator door, its paint chipped and faded. The only thing that set it apart was a faint, almost imperceptible scratching sound coming from behind it.

"Are you sure, Dean?" Kathryn asked, her eyebrows raised skeptically. "It's just a random choice."

"Hey, sometimes randomness is our best bet," he said with a shrug.

"Alright," Kathryn agreed, nodding her head.

As they approached the chosen elevator, Dean couldn't help but stare at the other players. He wondered whether any of them would make it out of this haunted hotel. Only time would tell.

"Ready?" he asked Kathryn as they stood before the elevator door, their hearts racing.

"Ready," she replied. Together, they pressed the elevator button, and the eerie melody from the intercom seemed to grow louder, echoing through the lobby.

The elevator doors creaked open, revealing a small, dimly lit space covered in cobwebs and dusty velvet wallpaper. Dean hesitated, but Kathryn stepped forward.

"Come on, Dean," she said, glancing back at him. "We've got to get back home."

Two other players, a girl around their age with fiery red hair and a tall, lanky boy, joined them as they entered the elevator. The doors shut behind them with a resounding thud, sealing them off from the grand lobby and its eerie atmosphere.

"Hey, I'm Alice," the redhead introduced herself. "And this is my cousin, Ben."

"Nice to meet you," Dean said.

"Same here," Kathryn echoed, exchanging a quick glance with her brother.

As the elevator began to ascend with a groan, Dean asked the newcomers, "So, how long have you guys been in the game?"

"Feels like forever," Ben answered, nervously. "We've been stuck on the same level for days now."

"Days?" Kathryn gasped, sharing a worried look with Dean.

"Yep," Alice said, crossing her arms with a sigh. "But we're not giving up. We're gonna find our way out of this hotel, no

matter what it takes."

"Us too," Dean said.

As the elevator came to an abrupt halt,

the doors creaked open, revealing a dark

bellhop or hotel manager's desk with

luggage carts on the side. A fireplace

crackled with a weak flame nearby.

One by one, they stepped out into the

darkness, leaving behind the relative safety

of the elevator as they ventured deeper into

the haunted hotel's unknown depths. The air

was colder, heavier, and it seemed to press

down on them as they moved forward,

guided only by the faint beam of light from

Ben's flashlight.

"Stay close," Dean whispered. "We don't know what we'll find in here."

"Or what might find us," Kathryn added. She wished she could see more than just a few feet in front of her, but the darkness was too thick.

"Right," Alice agreed, her voice quivering slightly. "We need to stick together, no matter what happens."

Dean tried to open the next door, but it was locked. "Alright," Dean said, taking a deep breath. "Let's look for a key."

Alice climbed over the luggage cart and rifled through the drawers. She held up a key, triumphantly waving it. "Found it!"

Dean took the key and unlocked the next door.

As they continued to navigate the shadowy corridors, the weight of the darkness seemed to grow heavier, pressing down upon them like a suffocating blanket. But the four players pressed forward.

The eerie silence in the haunted hotel sent chills down their spines. The darkness that surrounded them seemed almost alive, swallowing their whispered voices.

"Let's try this room first," Dean whispered, pointing to a door that creaked open when he lightly pushed it. They stepped inside, the air thick with dust and the scent of decay.

"Yuck, it smells like something died in here," Kathryn muttered, covering her nose with her sleeve.

"Alright, guys," Dean said, trying to keep his voice steady. "Let's start searching for clues. Anything that might help us get out of this place."

The four players split up, each one examining a different part of the room. Dean rifled through a desk drawer, finding nothing but old pens and scraps of paper.

"Hey, guys," Alice called out quietly, her voice trembling. "I found a library book on this shelf. It looks like it has some sort of code written in the margin."

"Great!" Dean said. "Bring it over here, and let's see if we can decipher it."

As Alice approached, Ben pulled open another drawer, revealing a small, tarnished key. "Guys, look at this skeleton key," he said, holding it up.

"Nice find!" Dean said. "That might just be our ticket out of here."

With the book and the key in hand, the players regrouped and began to piece together their findings. They had taken only a few steps back into the dark hallway when they heard a distant growl, echoing through the hotel like an ominous warning.

"Did you guys hear that?" Kathryn whispered.

"Yeah," Dean replied, trying to sound braver than he felt. "But we can't let it stop us. We're going to figure this out, whatever it takes."

As they continued to explore the haunted hotel, the eerie atmosphere weighed heavily on their shoulders. Shadows flickered around them, and the distant growls and screeches of unseen creatures fueled their fear.

"Guys, what if we never find our way out?" Alice asked, her voice trembling.

"Hey, don't think like that," Dean reassured her. "We'll find a way to beat the game."

"Dean's right," Kathryn chimed in. "We just need to keep looking for clues and stay together."

"Have you found any useful items during your time here, Ben?" Dean asked.

"Nothing useful," Ben replied, shaking his head. "Just some random objects that don't seem to help much, except for the Crucifix. It protects you against Seek and other entities."

"*Seek*?" Dean asked.

Ben's eyes grew wide, and his voice cracked as he told about the mysterious black creature that spawns from right out of the carpet.

"He's the worst. You're going down a long hallway and suddenly you hear the fast music, and you hear him breathing, growling, and then running like mad behind you. It's the scariest thing," Ben said. He began to breathe heavy with panic just thinking about it.

"What is it?" Kathryn asked.

"I don't know. Something dark and really mean. I don't want to talk about it anymore," Ben said and started walking down the hallway.

"Alright, guys," Dean said. "We've got each other's backs, right?"

"Definitely," Kathryn agreed, looking around for entities.

"No tripping the other person to escape the monsters, right?" Ben said.

"You mean people actually do that?" Kathryn asked with a shocked look on her face.

"Yeah, in zombie games sometimes. That way you can get away while the zombie eats your friend," Ben explained with a slight grin on his face.

"Disgusting... I don't want to hear anymore," Kathryn said.

As they moved cautiously through the dark corridors of the haunted hotel, their footsteps echoed softly against the aged walls, making them feel as if the very building was whispering secrets to them.

"Okay, let's think this through," Dean suggested, pausing to assess their situation. "If we're going to survive and find our way out, we need to stick together and help each other."

"Right," Kathryn nodded. "That means sharing any clues or items we find and watching each other's backs."

"Exactly," Ben agreed. "I've been at this longer than you guys, and I can tell you that teamwork is our best shot."

"Plus, it makes this creepy place a little less scary," Alice said.

As they ventured deeper into the hotel, the eerie silence was occasionally interrupted by distant creaks and unsettling noises. With every step, their senses were heightened, alert to any sign of danger.

"Hey, Dean," Kathryn whispered, her eyes darting around the dimly lit hallway. "Do you have any idea what we should be looking for? Clues, keys, anything?"

"Good question," Dean said, his brow furrowing in thought. "Well, we know we need to find a way out, so maybe there's some sort of master key, or a code to unlock the elevator room."

"The elevator room?" Kathryn asked. "How you do you know about an elevator room?"

"I heard some people talking about this game at school. They said the elevator room is the only way out," Dean said.

"Or maybe there's a hidden exit," Ben suggested.

"Let's keep our eyes peeled for anything out of the ordinary," Alice said, her gaze sweeping across the dusty floor and cobweb-covered walls.

"Wait, listen!" Kathryn suddenly whispered, pressing a finger to her lips.

The group froze, straining to hear the faint sound that had caught her attention. As the noise grew louder, it became clear that they were not alone in the haunted hotel.

A low growl reverberated through the dark corridor, making the hairs on the back of Dean's neck stand up. The flickering lights above them cast eerie shadows on the walls.

"Did you guys hear that?" Dean asked.

"Yeah," Alice whispered, her eyes wide with fear. "It sounded like some kind of...growling."

Dean couldn't shake the feeling that something was lurking nearby. He strained his ears, listening for any sign of movement or indication of what might be making the unnerving sound.

"Okay, let's keep moving," he said. "Stay alert and stick together."

As they inched their way down the hallway, the growls grew louder and more frequent. The flickering lights seemed to dance in sync with the menacing sounds.

"Dean, I don't like this," Kathryn murmured. "What if we're walking right into a trap?"

"Look, we've got no choice but to keep going," Dean answered, his heart pounding in his chest. "We need to find a way out, remember?"

"Right," she nodded, taking a deep breath.

Just as they turned the corner, the lights went out completely, plunging them into darkness. A sudden gust of wind blew

30

past them, followed by a distorted, guttural growl that echoed throughout the haunted hotel.

"Guys, I think we have a problem," Ben stammered, his voice quivering with fear.

"Rush," Alice whispered, her face pale as she stared into the darkness. "It's here."

As panic set in, Dean tried to think of a plan, but his thoughts were interrupted by a faint creaking noise coming from the end of the hallway. Squinting through the darkness, he could barely make out the outline of a large cabinet, its door's rusty hinges squeaking as it slowly swung open. There were three other large cabinets in the hallway, too.

"Quick, everyone! Into the cabinets!" Dean yelled. "We need to hide now!"

The kids each jumped into a wooden cabinet and shut the doors. Lights flickered feverishly and the guttural growl of Rush raged outside their cabinets, rattling the doors with its power.

Kathryn held in a scream as she saw the dark figure pass by the crack of light in her cabinet door. Dean closed his eyes and tried to think of something nice like chocolate ice cream or birthday cake. Alice shivered and stared as the creature passed her cabinet. Ben looked on with a dead eyed look like he'd been through this situation one too many times.

Finally, Rush left the room and all was quiet. The kids climbed out of their cabinets and sprinted down the corridor, the growls and flickering lights intensifying behind them. Just as they reached the threshold of another mysterious room, yet another ominous presence loomed over them, its evil grin almost visible in the dark.

Chapter 3.

Dean squinted into the darkness. Shadows crept along the peeling wallpaper of the abandoned hotel room. A single bulb flickered overhead.

"I don't like this," Kathryn whispered, moving closer to her brother. "We need to get out of this game."

Kathryn and Dean moved cautiously through the decrepit hotel, peering into each dusty room. Shadows shifted in the dim light, playing tricks on their eyes.

"Did you see that?" Kathryn gasped, clutching her brother's arm.

Dean shook his head. "Just our imagination. Come on."

They entered what was once an elegant ballroom. Shredded satin curtains swayed in a phantom breeze. The crystal chandelier overhead creaked ominously.

Kathryn shivered. "This place gives me the creeps."

"Tell me about it." Dean tried the balcony doors but they were stuck fast. He jimmied the rusty latch with his table leg.

Suddenly, a blood-curdling shriek pierced the air. Kathryn yelped, startled.

Dean whirled around. "What was that?"

The chandelier began to rock violently. Kathryn pointed a trembling finger upwards. "Dean, look out!"

Dean dove to the floor just as the chandelier plummeted down, shattering into a million shards with an earsplitting crash.

Heart pounding, Dean helped Kathryn up. "You okay?"

She nodded, wide-eyed. "That was close!"

Dean grimaced. "Too close. We need to get out of here before this whole place comes crashing down."

With renewed urgency, they hurried from the ruined ballroom, hoping to find safety before the hotel claimed them as its next victims.

Kathryn and Dean crept down a long hallway lined with peeling floral wallpaper. Faded room numbers hung crookedly on each warped door.

"Maybe one of these rooms has a fire escape we could use," Kathryn whispered hopefully.

Behind a half-open door, Kathryn spotted a dusty piano. She tiptoed inside and tapped out a few notes, wincing at the jarring sound.

Dean poked his head in. "Find something?"

"Just this old piano," she said. "Keep looking."

Exhausted, they regrouped with Ben and Alice in the hall. Kathryn slumped against the wall. "We've searched everywhere. I don't think there's a way out."

Dean squeezed her shoulder reassuringly. "There's always a way. We just have to stay sharp."

Reenergized by her brother's optimism, Kathryn pushed off from the wall. "You're right. Let's keep trying."

Suddenly, the lights in the hallway began to flicker. An eerie, distorted growling sound echoed through the air.

Kathryn's eyes widened. "What was that?"

Dean grabbed her hand. "It's Rush. We need to hide, now!"

They sprinted down the hall, darting glances back and forth for a hiding spot. Up ahead, Dean spotted a small closet nestled between two rooms.

"In here!" He pulled open the door and ushered Kathryn inside. Dean held his breath, listening intently as the growling grew louder.

The growling turned into a roar as Rush sped into view, its hulking form barely visible in the dim light. It hovered menacingly, drifting from room to room, breaking light bulbs as it went.

After what seemed like an eternity, the sounds faded into the distance. Dean let out a shaky breath. "I think it's gone."

He cracked open the closet door. The hallway was empty, scattered with broken glass that crunched under their feet as they emerged.

Kathryn exhaled in relief. "That was way too close."

Dean nodded, eyes scanning the hall warily. "No kidding. Let's keep moving."

With Rush's chilling presence fresh in their minds, the two pressed on.

They moved cautiously through the corridor, senses alert for any sign of the next threat. Dean kept one hand on the wall, guiding them in the dim light.

"I don't like this," Kathryn whispered. "It's too quiet now."

Dean nodded. "I know. But we have to keep going."

They came to an intersection where the hall split in two directions. Dean paused, considering.

"Which way?" Kathryn asked.

Before Dean could respond, a soft voice sounded behind them.

"Psst."

They whirled around. There, hovering at the end of the corridor, was a shadowy figure. Glowing eyes peered from beneath a dark hood.

Kathryn gasped and grabbed Dean's arm. He stood frozen, fighting the urge to meet the creature's gaze.

"Don't look at it," he said under his breath. "That must be Screech."

The figure drifted closer. "Psst," it hissed again.

Dean's heart pounded. He tried to think. Screech could hurt them if they looked at it. But it might also attack if they didn't.

Making a split-second decision, he turned and pulled Kathryn around the corner, breaking eye contact.

"Run!" he yelled.

They sprinted down the left passageway, Screech's chilling presence at their backs. Still, they had survived another encounter.

They ran blindly, not daring to glance behind them. Dean's mind raced. How could they escape Screech without looking at it?

Suddenly, he noticed a door up ahead. Grabbing Kathryn's hand, he yanked it open and pulled them both inside. They found themselves in a dusty room, surrounded by shelves stacked with boxes and supplies.

They looked back. The door was silent.

"They can't pass through if the door closes," Dean said.

"Phew, that was close," Kathryn whispered once the immediate danger had passed.

Dean nodded, though his forehead creased with worry. "We can't keep running and hiding forever. We've got to find a way to beat these monsters."

Kathryn bit her lip. "But how? Nothing seems to stop them for long."

Dean thought for a moment. "What we need is a trap of some kind. If we could lure Screech into the right spot, maybe we could contain it."

"A trap?" Kathryn looked doubtful. "I don't know..."

"We have to try something," Dean said firmly. "Come on, let's take a look around this room. There's got to be something we can use."

They began cautiously searching the shelves and boxes, the first sparks of a plan forming in Dean's inventive mind. If they were clever enough, perhaps they could turn the hunters into the hunted.

Kathryn rummaged through the boxes, not finding much of use. Some old books, spare lightbulbs, rolls of duct tape. She sighed.

"This is hopeless. There's nothing here we can use against those monsters."

Dean didn't answer right away. He was staring thoughtfully at one of the shelves.

"Not necessarily," Ben said. He grabbed a crucifix.

Kathryn looked skeptical. "You really think we can scare them away with that?"

"It works on Dracula in the movies," Ben said.

Before long, an ominous "Psst..." sounded from the darkness. Screech was close by.

Kathryn and Dean hid behind a corner, hearts pounding. This had to work. It was their only chance to gain some control over

this nightmarish game.

Chapter 4.

The door to the dusty storage room creaked open. Ben poked his head out and glanced warily down the hallway.

"I don't know about this," he whispered to Alice. "Dean doesn't really seem to have any idea where we're going in this place."

Alice nodded, her eyes wide. "Yeah, we keep running into more of those freaky monsters. Like that Screech thing. My neck's still sore from where it bit me." She rubbed the red marks on her neck ruefully.

"Exactly," said Ben. "I say we ditch Dean and Kathryn and go off on our own. We can't keep blindly following them, hoping they'll lead us out of here."

Alice bit her lip. "You're right. We need to take matters into our own hands." She met Ben's gaze. "But we should agree to find each other again if one of us does make it out first. Deal?"

"Deal," Ben agreed, holding out his hand to shake on it. As their hands clasped, a blood-curdling screech echoed down the hallway, making them both jump. Ben's heart pounded wildly in his chest.

"Let's get out of here before Screech catches our scent again," Alice said urgently.

Ben nodded, wiping his sweaty palms on his jeans. They slipped out of the storage room and hurried off down the hall, disappearing around a corner just as Dean and Kathryn emerged from the doorway opposite. Neither pair noticed the other as they ventured deeper into the menacing hotel, intent on finding their own way out.

Dean watched as Ben and Alice disappeared around the corner, an uneasy feeling settling in his gut. He had hoped they would all stick together. Dean noticed something glistening on the floor. Ben had dropped the crucifix. He picked it up and placed it in his pocket.

"Come on," Kathryn said, tugging at his sleeve. "Let's try this way."

Dean took a deep breath and turned to the door across from them. It was tall and ominous, with peeling gray paint and a tarnished metal handle. He grasped it firmly and pulled it open. Beyond was a long, dimly lit hallway that seemed to stretch on forever. The occasional flickering light cast weird shadows across the stained carpet and chipped walls.

Kathryn stepped closer to Dean as they began walking slowly down the hall. Their footsteps seemed unnaturally loud in the heavy silence. Dean's senses were on high alert, his muscles tensed and ready to react. Out of the corner of his eye, he thought he saw one of the shadows move, but when he whipped his head around there was nothing.

"I don't like this place," Kathryn whispered, her voice quavering slightly.

"Me neither, but we don't have a choice. Come on, stay close." Dean put a protective arm around her shoulders as they continued onward, deeper into the darkness.

They had only gone a little further when Kathryn said, "Do you hear that?" Dean strained his ears. At first all he could hear was the buzzing of the dim lights, but then another sound came through. It was faint but unmistakable - a weird, fast-paced music seeming to come out of the very walls.

As they walked slowly forward, the music got louder and more chaotic. Kathryn's grip on Dean's arm tightened. He felt his own heart begin to race in his chest.

Suddenly Kathryn gasped and pointed ahead of them. "Dean, look!"

Dean followed her gaze and felt his blood run cold. There, spaced out along the hallway walls, were disembodied eyeballs. They stared straight ahead, unblinking, seeming to follow Dean and Kathryn as they passed by. The effect was deeply unsettling.

"What is this place?" Kathryn whispered.

Dean shook his head, at a loss for words. The music swelled around them as more eyeballs appeared, keeping pace with their steps. Dean couldn't shake the feeling that they were being watched, and not just by the eyes.

Something was coming.

Without warning, the carpet right behind them began to bulge and ripple. Dean and Kathryn spun around just as a dark, writhing mass erupted from the floor. It rose up, forming into the twisted shape of Seek. Its slimy black body towered over them, undulating and pulsing. At its apex was the giant, bloodshot eye, rolling in its socket before fixing on the two kids.

Kathryn screamed. Dean yelled "Run!"

They took off down the hallway, Seek

oozing after them. The eyeballs embedded

in the walls seemed to follow their progress.

Hideous arms and hands reached out from

the shattered windows, grasping at Dean

and Kathryn as they sprinted past.

Kathryn tripped over an overturned

chair, crashing to the floor. "Kathryn!" Dean

yelled. He hauled her up by the arms just as

Seek's shadow fell over them. They dodged

around a corner, the sound of Seek's raspy

breaths echoing behind.

Dean's heart hammered against his

ribs as they raced through room after room,

leaping over debris and around maze-like

corners. He could hear Seek gaining on them, its oily, heavy body slapping against the floor as it pursued them.

Dean's mind raced as he caught his breath. He had to think of something, fast.

His hand brushed against the crucifix in his pocket. The crucifix!

"I have an idea," Dean said. He pulled out the crucifix.

Kathryn's eyes went wide. "Do you think that will stop it?"

"I hope so. Help me prop this chair under the doorknob."

They barricaded the door as best they could. Dean took a deep breath and faced the entrance, crucifix held out before him.

The pounding against the door intensified. The wood began to splinter and crack.

"Get behind me," Dean said. Kathryn huddled against the back wall.

With a final crash, the door burst open. Seek oozed into the room, writhing and pulsing. Its eye fixed on Dean. It bounded toward Dean with full force and speed.

Dean stood his ground. As Seek rushed toward him, he thrust the crucifix forward.

Blinding white light erupted from the crucifix. Glowing chains materialized in the air, wrapping around Seek. The creature let out an unearthly wail as the chains bound it tight, rooting it to the floor.

"It's working!" Kathryn cried.

Dean kept the crucifix aimed at Seek. "Go, now!" he yelled.

Kathryn ran through the next doorway. Dean backed out after her, crucifix still extended. Dean threw the crucifix at the creature and ran through the doorway.

Seek's enraged screeches echoed behind them. The glowing chains held fast.

Kathryn leaned against the wall, catching her breath. Her heart was pounding.

"That was way too close," she said. "I really thought we were goners."

"For a second there, so did I," he admitted. "But we made it."

The door behind them turned red and Seek pounded on it furiously, but it couldn't get through.

"Let's get out of here," Dean said.

Kathryn nodded. The eerie music still echoed through the halls, raising the hairs on the back of her neck.

"Let's keep moving," Dean said. "Ben and Alice could be in trouble."

Side by side, they walked deeper into the darkness.

Chapter 5.

The dusty library enveloped Dean as he entered through Door #50. Cobwebs draped across towering shelves like abandoned lace curtains. He brushed a strand of web from his face and squinted through the dim light filtering in through grime-coated windows.

Dean paused as a glint of gold caught his eye. Crouching down, he found a small scrap of paper tucked behind a leaning stack of books. Strange symbols marked the page

- Roman numerals and astrological signs that made no sense together.

"What is this?" Dean muttered, turning the paper over in his hands. It wasn't a page torn from a book. The paper felt old, but the ink looked freshly scribbled. Like a code.

A secret code, hidden in the library? He glanced around warily, but the room remained still and silent. Slipping the paper into his pocket, Dean moved further into the library. Each shelf he passed loomed over him, shrouded in cobwebs that swayed ever so slightly in the stale air.

Kathryn peered down the dusty aisles of books, anxiety prickling her skin. "Where could they be?" she whispered to Dean.

Her brother shook his head, shoulders tense. This library was like a labyrinth - all twisting shelves and hidden rooms. Ben and Alice could be anywhere.

Kathryn hurried ahead, glancing down each aisle. A flash of movement caught her eye. She turned, squinting into the shadows. Was that...?

"Ben! Alice!" Kathryn shouted, sprinting toward two familiar figures hunched over a table.

Ben's head jerked up, eyes wide. "Kathryn?"

Kathryn crashed into them, nearly toppling a teetering pile of books. She threw her arms around their necks. "You're okay!"

Alice squeaked in surprise, then laughed. "It's good to see you too."

Dean jogged up behind Kathryn. "Where have you guys been? We've been looking all over."

Ben straightened, brushing dust off a leatherbound book. "Sorry. We got caught up in research."

"Research?" Kathryn tilted her head.

"We think these books have codes in them," Alice said eagerly. "Codes that might help us escape."

Dean frowned. "And you couldn't have left us a note or something?"

Ben shrugged sheepishly. "Didn't want Figure to find it."

"You mean you didn't want Figure to figure it out," Kathryn joked.

"Lame joke award," Dean teased.

"So, what's the plan?" Kathryn asked.

Alice said, "We hunt for codes."

They nodded in agreement. Kathryn's enthusiasm faded as she studied their tired faces.

"Are you guys, okay?" Kathryn asked. "This place is creepy. I was scared when we got separated."

Alice offered a reassuring smile. "We're alright. Just trying to solve this puzzle."

Ben nodded. "Figure's still out there, but we're safe for now."

She met their eyes. "Please stick together from now on. No more splitting up," Kathryn said. Ben and Alice nodded. "Let's find those codes!"

They searched for the book codes. The keys to escape were here somewhere, hidden in ink and pages.

"Tell us what you know so far," Dean said. "I don't understand this code box." There was a lockbox on the door with combination dials and strange symbols and Roman numerals.

Ben's eyes lit up as he explained the code machine. "I figured out how to use this thing. My friend Josh showed me a trick for cracking locker combinations back home. This machine works the same way."

He held up the strange device, covered in dials and buttons. Kathryn leaned in, intrigued.

"See, it needs a five-digit code to open the next door. We just have to find number combinations hidden in these books."

Dean's eyebrows shot up. "Hidden codes? In books?"

Ben nodded eagerly. "Yeah, watch."

He grabbed a book off the shelf, flipping through the pages. "The library books have symbols in them. Put together, they make a five-digit code."

His finger traced the musty pages.
"Like here – a triangle. Then on this page, a circle."

"This is just like a secret treasure hunt," Kathryn said.

"Only you would be excited about homework, Kathryn," said Dean.

She smirked. Books were her happy place.

Ben smiled and followed her. They flipped through book after book down aisle after aisle. The promise of mystery made this ghostly library a lot less scary.

Kathryn eagerly grabbed an armful of books and plopped down at a table. She was totally in her element, combing through page after page for hidden clues.

"Hey, check this out," Ben whispered. He pointed up at the wall, where a tarnished plaque read 'Door 50.'

"Door 50? What's so special about that?" Dean asked.

Ben's eyes glinted mischievously. "Rumor has it, behind Door 50 is a secret shop called the Jeff Shop."

Kathryn looked up from her book, intrigued. "A secret shop? I wonder what they sell."

"Probably something to help us with these crazy rooms. Like a key or useful item."

Dean folded his arms. "Or it could be a trap. I don't trust anything in this place."

They gazed at the imposing door apprehensively. A faint scratching sound came from the other side, making them jump.

Chapter 6.

After several minutes of fruitless hunting, Kathryn let out a frustrated sigh. "This is impossible! There must be thousands of books here."

As he spoke, a low guttural growl echoed through the library's vast interior. Kathryn and Dean exchanged an uneasy glance.

"What was that?" Kathryn whispered.

The growl sounded again, louder this time. Heavy footsteps followed, the floorboards creaking under some immense weight.

"Something's in here with us," she breathed.

Dean swallowed hard, peering down the shadowy aisles. The footsteps grew nearer, accompanied by a raspy snuffling. Dean's heart pounded.

"Stay behind me," he told Kathryn, edging forward. "We need to keep looking while avoiding...whatever that thing is."

Kathryn nodded, sticking close as they continued to search the shelves. The ominous sounds continued, making the hairs on Dean's neck stand up.

Dean froze as a massive, misshapen figure lumbered into view at the end of the aisle. It stood on two gangly legs that bent backwards at the knees, its torso hunched over. Where its head should have been was a giant, gaping mouth ringed by jagged teeth.

Kathryn stifled a shriek. "It's the Figure," she whispered.

The Figure's mouth gaped open and a long, showing rows of sharp teeth. It had no eyes, but seemed to sense their presence, turning its head in their direction.

Dean reacted fast, pulling Kathryn down to crouch behind a bookshelf. They held perfectly still, hardly daring to breathe as the Figure shuffled closer.

The Figure was close now. Dean spotted a book jutting out from the shelf at his eye level. An intricate symbol was etched into the worn leather cover - one of the books they sought! Carefully, slowly, he eased it from the shelf, praying the movement wouldn't catch the creature's attention.

The book came free without a sound. The Figure paused; head tilted. Then it turned and continued its patrol down the aisle.

Dean let out a shaky breath of relief.

"That was close," Kathryn whispered.

Dean nodded, holding up the leather book. "But we got one."

"The coast is clear. Let's keep looking," Dean said.

They moved carefully through the dusty aisles, senses alert for any sound of the Figure's return. More decrepit books lined the shelves, their titles faded with age. Cobwebs draped across the books like shrouds. This library felt ancient, as if it had been sealed away and forgotten long ago.

Kathryn paused, squinting at a shelf ahead. "There's another one!" She darted forward and snatched a book bound in cracked green leather. An elaborate symbol marked its cover to match the paper Dean

had found.

Chapter 7.

D ean crept through the dusty library, flashlight in hand. Cobwebs draped across the bookshelves like veils, and the air smelled of mildew and mothballs. Kathryn followed close behind, her eyes darting around nervously.

"This place gives me the creeps," Kathryn whispered.

Dean swept his flashlight across the rows of books. "Let's just find those code books and get out of here."

They hurried down the aisles, scanning the shelves. The old books all had the same faded leather spines, indistinguishable from one another. Dean's palms began to sweat. They were running out of time. Figure could be lurking anywhere.

Kathryn gave a startled yelp as a spider scuttled across her shoe. Dean stifled a laugh.

"It's just a tiny spider," he said.

"I know, I know," Kathryn grumbled, shaking the spider off her shoe. "This place is freaking me out, that's all."

Dean playfully tossed a wad of cobweb at her, eliciting an angry scowl.

"Just a tiny spider. What harm could it be?" he said, laughing.

Then the spider jumped at Dean's face. He tossed it aside and hid behind the bookshelf. He looked back at the spider only to see it climbing nimbly across the floor.

"That's Timothy," Ben said. "He can damage you, but only a little."

"I do feel a bit weaker," Dean said, brushing cobwebs off his shoulder.

After several tense minutes of searching, Kathryn's face lit up. "Here's one!" She pulled a book off the shelf, blowing dust off the cover.

Dean hurried over. "Only six more to go."

They scoured every shelf, nook, and cranny until each code book was found. Dean let out a sigh of relief. "Let's get out of this creepy place."

Kathryn nodded eagerly, clutching the books to her chest.

They approached the ornate door at the end of the hallway. This was it - the moment they had been searching for. Kathryn held the code books tightly, her knuckles turning white. Ben and Alice watched anxiously.

Dean's palms were slick with sweat as he studied the intricate lock. It required a specific code from each of the eight books to open. Somewhere in this haunted hotel, the grotesque Figure lurked. They had to work quickly.

Kathryn flipped through the books, scanning for the codes printed in glowing ink on certain pages. She showed Dean each one. He began turning the lock's dials carefully.

Click. Click. Click. Only halfway there. Dean's hands shook slightly. He couldn't mess this up.

Suddenly, a blood-curdling roar echoed down the hallway. Figure had found them. Dean's stomach dropped.

"Hurry!" Kathryn urged, her face pale.

Dean's fingers flew, dialing in the remaining codes. Just as the towering creature careened around the corner, arms outstretched, the lock clicked open.

Dean wrenched the door open and all the kids dove through, slamming it shut behind them. Made it by the skin of their teeth. But they couldn't relax yet.

Kathryn leaned against the heavy door. That was way too close for comfort. If Dean had been just a few seconds slower with that lock...she shuddered at the thought.

Dean let out a shaky breath. "Nice job finding those codes."

Kathryn managed a faint smile, though her legs still felt like jelly. "I can't believe we actually got away from that thing."

They took a moment to survey their new surroundings. The room appeared to be some kind of store, though it was just as dim and dusty as the rest of this creepy hotel. Shelves were lined with odd trinkets, candles, and various tools.

"Where are we?" Dean whispered. Something about this place made him want to keep his voice down.

Kathryn picked up an old lamp from a shelf and turned it on. As the light flickered over the room, they both gasped. Behind the counter stood two figures - a skeleton wearing a top hat and holding a cane, and a short goblin-like creature with green skin and yellow eyes.

"Welcome to the Jeff Shop," the skeleton rasped in an ancient, creaky voice. "I'm Bob and this is my friend El Goblino. We're here to help you on your quest."

Kathryn and Dean exchanged amazed looks. This adventure just kept getting stranger...

"Help us?" Dean said cautiously. "How do you know about our quest?"

"We know many things," Bob replied mysteriously. "We've been waiting for you."

El Goblino nodded eagerly. "Yes yes! You must defeat the evil that dwells here. We have tools that can help."

Dean looked over the odd assortment of items around the shop. His eyes landed on a silver crucifix glinting under the lamp light.

"How much for this?" Dean asked, picking it up.

"For you, 300 gold," said Bob. "It will be most helpful."

Dean clasped the crucifix, feeling a sense of protection emanating from it. "I used one that I found earlier in the game. It definitely helped us."

Kathryn's eyes scanned the shelves, looking for anything else that might prove useful. Her gaze landed on an ornate skeleton key glinting under the lamp light.

"Ooh, what about this?" She asked, picking it up.

Bob nodded approvingly. "An excellent choice. That skeleton key can open any lock in this hotel. It will serve you well," he said. "After all, it's my favorite item" As he laughed, his bones jiggled and his teeth chattered.

Kathryn grinned and added the key to her pocket. Next to it, she spotted a heavy-duty flashlight.

"And this flashlight too, please," she said. "I have a feeling we'll be venturing into some dark places soon."

"Smart thinking," said El Goblino. "The darkness hides many secrets in this place."

Kathryn clicked on the flashlight, testing its bright beam. With the skeleton key and flashlight, she felt better prepared for the unknown perils ahead.

"Thank you both, truly," she said to Bob and El Goblino. "I don't know how we'd get through this without your help."

"It is our duty and honor," said Bob with a bow.

"And we like the gold!" El Goblino admitted, giggling. His eyes glowed. "Now go bravely. The keys and the final door await!"

Clutching their new tools, Kathryn and Dean waved farewell to their unexpected allies. The real quest was just beginning...

Kathryn and Dean stepped out of the eerie storefront, back into the dimly lit hallway.

"Alright, where to next?" Kathryn asked, switching on her flashlight to pierce the darkness ahead.

Dean consulted the tattered map he'd found earlier. "Looks like we need to head to the greenhouse. Then the electrical room after that."

Together they crept down the hallway, senses alert for any sign of the hotel's lurking horrors. Kathryn's beam swept side to side, illuminating cobwebs and age-worn carpet.

Dean paused, holding up a hand. "Did you hear that?" he whispered.

A skittering, scratching sound echoed from around the corner. Kathryn froze, flashlight fixed ahead.

The scratching intensified, accompanied by an ominous hiss. Kathryn's heart hammered against her ribs. What fresh terror awaited them now? She exchanged an anxious look with Dean. Gripping her flashlight like a weapon, Kathryn steadied herself.

Chapter 8.

Kathryn stepped out into the courtyard, blinking against the sudden sunlight. The courtyard was an oasis of green, with vines crawling up ancient stone walls and flowers bursting from every crevice.

"Kathryn!" Ben jogged up to her, relief breaking across his face. "I'm so glad I found you."

Kathryn smiled back, feeling the knot in her chest loosen. She wasn't alone in this twisted game anymore. "Me too. We'll have a much better chance getting through this together."

Ben nodded, his eyes alert for hidden threats.

Her eyes caught on a statue in the center of the courtyard. An angel with wings outstretched, carved from smooth white stone. She grabbed Ben's arm. "Look, we should use that statue as a meeting point if we get separated again."

Ben frowned. "Hopefully it won't come to that. But good idea." He paused. "Have you noticed anything...strange about this place?"

Kathryn shook her head. "Other than being trapped in a deadly game? No, everything seems normal." She forced a laugh.

Ben didn't smile back. His expression remained tense, eyes darting around.

Kathryn felt unease trickle down her spine. What did Ben know that she didn't? She was about to ask when a distant howl split the air.

They both jumped. "We need to move," Ben said grimly. Together they hurried down a stone pathway.

"It's so peaceful here," Kathryn murmured. "Hard to believe this is all part of that awful hotel."

Ben nodded, also taking in their surroundings. "We should rest."

They settled on a stone bench. "So, what's the plan?" she asked Ben. "For getting through the Greenhouse in one piece?"

"I heard from other players that there are three main threats in the Greenhouse: Rush, Eyes, and Screech," Ben said.

Kathryn shuddered at the eerie names. "What are they?"

"Rush is some kind of shadow creature. It floats and makes the lights flicker before an attack. 'Eyes' is a floating mass of actual eyeballs that can hurt you if you make eye contact." Ben grimaced. "And Screech...well the name says it all. Emits an awful high-pitched sound."

Kathryn bit her lip nervously. "So how do we handle them?"

"Carefully. Work together. Don't panic." Ben said.

Kathryn managed a small smile, despite her lingering doubts. "Right. Teamwork."

A distant growl rumbled through the trees. Kathryn jumped to her feet, peering into the shadows.

"Let's get back to the door," Ben said urgently. "Dean and Alice are probably waiting."

Kathryn followed Ben down the stone path, towards Door #90 where Dean and Alice awaited. She tried to focus on their plan of sticking together, watching each other's backs, communicating. But an uneasy feeling gnawed at her.

Ben seemed to know so much already about the threats inside the Greenhouse. More than he should for someone new to the game. She studied him from the corner of her eye as they walked. His jaw was tense, his eyes constantly scanning their surroundings. He looked...guilty. Like he was hiding something.

Kathryn's steps slowed. "Ben," she began hesitantly. "Have you...been here before? To the Greenhouse?"

Ben's pace didn't falter. "No. I told you, I just heard things."

"From who?" Kathryn pressed.

"Other players."

"What other players?"

Ben exhaled sharply. "Does it matter?"

Kathryn grabbed his arm. "Yes, it matters! If you've been here before, if you know more than you're letting on..."

Ben wrenched his arm away. "I don't know anything, okay?" He glared at her. "Let's just focus on surviving."

He stalked off again down the path. Kathryn watched him, puzzled. Kathryn hurried to catch up to Ben.

As they rounded a bend in the path, Kathryn spotted a glint of metal nestled among some bushes. She darted over and extracted a tarnished skeleton key, its teeth jagged and worn.

"Hey, check this out!" she called to Ben excitedly. "A skeleton key - this could come in handy."

Ben nodded, peering at the key. "Great find. Let's hope it opens whatever doors we come across next."

Buoyed by the discovery, Kathryn resumed searching the surroundings. In the hollow of an old tree, she noticed a stubby candle tucked away.

"And a candle too," she mused, picking it up. "Could be useful if we end up somewhere dark." Also, she pocketed a rusty lockpick.

She stowed the items in her backpack for safekeeping. As she did, her fingers brushed against the cool plastic of the bottle of vitamins she'd picked up earlier.

Kathryn hesitated, then pulled out the bottle to show Ben. "I found these vitamins back earlier. No idea if they'll actually help us or if it's just part of the game. But maybe we should hold onto them?"

Ben shrugged. "Couldn't hurt." His voice trailed off as a distant but unmistakable growl rumbled through the air.

Without another word, they hurried back to the stone walkway, looking around for any signs of approaching creatures. The door to the Greenhouse waited ahead. And whatever horrors lay within.

Kathryn's heart pounded as she and Ben rushed back to the stone walkway. Still, Kathryn's mind raced with questions. What awaited them beyond the door? Would the four of them be enough to handle it? And what about Ben - could he really be trusted?

Their footsteps echoed on the stones as they reached the doorway where Dean and Alice stood.

"Took you long enough," Dean said.

"We were talking about the monsters that appear in the Greenhouse. Ben says there's at least three," Kathryn said.

Dean nodded and then said, "No telling what we'll find in there. But if we watch each other's backs, then we can do this."

He gripped the door handle. "Ready?"

They all nodded, and Dean wrenched open the door. The heavy air and earthy scent of the Greenhouse billowed out. Kathryn peered past him into the shadowy, overgrown space.

Here we go, she thought. Into the unknown once more.

Chapter 9.

Dean and Kathryn stepped into the Greenhouse. They slowly stepped further into the long dimly lit room filled with overgrown plants and eerie shadows.

"This is worse than I imagined," Kathryn whispered, her eyes darting around nervously.

"Stay close," Dean replied, his voice low but firm. "We've got to find the way to the electrical room. Unfortunately, this is the only way to Door #100."

As they cautiously made their way through the maze of twisting vines and thorny branches, they suddenly heard a horrific screeching sound.

"Uh, Dean?" Kathryn said, her voice trembling. "Do you hear that?"

"Shh, stay quiet," Dean whispered.

Just then, a grinning face with tentacles flashed in front of them. It was Screech.

"What is *that* thing?!" Kathryn exclaimed, taking a step back.

"Run!" Dean shouted, pulling her along as they bolted through the pathway of the Greenhouse.

"Where do we go?!" Kathryn cried, dodging around a towering mass of tangled vines.

"Anywhere but here!" Dean yelled back, his heart pounding in his chest.

As they raced through the dark Greenhouse, Dean could feel the force of Screech licking at his heels.

"Come on, Kathryn, we're almost there!" he shouted, urging her forward.

Despite the fear and uncertainty churning inside him, Dean refused to give up. He was determined to protect his sister and find a way out of this nightmare, no matter what it took.

"Okay, we're safe," he panted, finally emerging from the Greenhouse.

Kathryn nodded, her eyes wide with fear. "That was close. Too close."

"Tell me about it," Dean muttered, his mind already racing ahead to the next challenge they would face.

Kathryn leaned over, trying to catch her breath after their narrow escape.

"That thing almost got us," she said between gasps. "What are we gonna do?"

Dean scanned the area, his mind working furiously. "We need to keep moving. Staying in one place makes us an easy target."

Kathryn nodded, straightening up.

"You're right. Let's go this way."

She started to walk down a narrow path between towering hedges. Dean followed close behind, senses on high alert.

They hadn't gone more than a few steps when a screech pierced the air. Dean's blood turned to ice.

"It found us!" Kathryn cried.

"Run!" Dean yelled, shoving his sister forward.

They took off, feet pounding against the overgrown path. Dean's legs burned but he didn't dare slow down. Risking a glance back, he saw Screech's writhing tentacled form barreling toward them, screaming malevolently.

Suddenly, Ben appeared from between the hedges right in front of them. Before Dean could react, Ben stuck his foot out, tripping Kathryn. She fell hard, crying out in pain and shock.

"No!" Dean shouted, skidding to a stop. But it was too late. Screech loomed over them, blocking any chance of escape.

Kathryn looked up at Ben with anger and betrayal in her eyes.

"You tripped me!" she accused.

Ben just shrugged, not looking at all sorry. "It's every man for himself in here."

With that, he took off down a side path. Alice quickly followed behind him, not even sparing a glance back.

Dean's hands curled into fists. Screech's shadow fell over them and its screech reverberated through the greenhouse.

Thinking fast, Dean pulled out the crucifix he had bought from the Jeff Shop.

"Let's see if this works," he muttered. Gripping the crucifix, he thrust it toward Screech.

The creature recoiled, its screech turning into a wail. It froze in place, eyes darting around frantically.

"It's working!" Dean shouted. He grabbed Kathryn's arm, hauling her to her feet. "Come on, we gotta go!"

Supporting his sister, they took off down the path again. Dean kept one hand holding the crucifix behind them. He didn't know how long it would restrain Screech.

Kathryn winced as she ran on her twisted ankle but didn't complain. Her eyes were hard with anger.

"I can't believe Ben would do that," she said bitterly. "What a traitor."

Dean just nodded, focused on getting them to safety. But inwardly, his hands itched to get ahold of Ben. There would be a reckoning for his betrayal.

For now, though, escape was their only goal. Dean guided them left and right through the maze, the crucifix their only lifeline against the predator on their heels.

"This way!" he yelled, pulling Kathryn down a side path.

Kathryn coughed, struggling to breathe.

They had to get out of here. Spying a small gap between two flowering bushes, he shoved Kathryn through first and then squeezed in after her.

They found themselves in a small alcove. Kathryn leaned against the wall, wheezing.

"Just hang on," Dean told her. He peered out cautiously. The main path was engulfed in darkness. Going back was not an option.

Suddenly the screeching sounds stopped. Dean looked around wildly. Where was Screech? Had they lost the entity?

They no longer heard the screeching noise behind them.

"It's a trick. Get into one of the cabinets. Quick!" Dean yelled. He and Kathryn each jumped into cabinets that lined the wall.

Sure enough, Screech raced down the hallway with its wide, toothy grin on full display as it passed their storage cabinets.

When Screech was gone, Kathryn and Dean stepped out of the cabinets into a dimly lit hallway. The air was cool and damp, with droplets of moisture clinging to the stone walls.

Kathryn shivered, rubbing her hands over her arms. "Where to now?"

Dean studied the dark path ahead. "This way," he said. Kathryn hurried to catch up. The Greenhouse was getting darker.

"This way," he shouted, changing direction.

"It's so dark in here. I can hardly see anything," Kathryn said. Shafts of light shone down through holes in the roof, illuminating swirling dust.

"Where's that candle you found?"
Dean said, trying to catch his breath.

She handed it to Dean.

As they walked, Kathryn couldn't stop
replaying the greenhouse escape in her
mind. She saw Ben's foot shoot out, tripping
her up just as Screech was bearing down on
them.

"He meant to do it," she muttered
angrily.

Dean glanced back at her. "We don't
know for sure."

"Yes, we do!" Kathryn insisted. "He
wanted me to get caught. He's a traitor."

"Maybe," Dean said. "Or maybe he just
panicked."

The windows and stone walls seemed to shift and writhe in the flickering candlelight.

A few cabinets were on the left side of the Greenhouse walls.

"Stay close to the cabinets in case we need to hide," Dean said.

"I don't like this," Kathryn whispered.

"Me either," he replied.

As they walked in darkness, the candle's flame quivered and turned purple.

"Look, the candlelight is purple," Kathryn said.

"That's weird," Dean said. Then they both felt the heavy feeling of an entity nearby.

"I think it's a warning," Kathryn said.

A group of eyes gathered in front of them.

"Don't look at them!" yelled Dean. "Just keep running forward!"

They covered their eyes and ran blindly down the hallway until the ominous feeling of staring eyes was far behind them.

"I can't believe I didn't fall flat on my face," Kathryn said as they slowed down. "I don't even want to look back."

Dean did look back and said, "It's gone. We don't have much farther to go. See that light at the end of the hallway?" He pointed to a slight slant of light coming from beneath a closed door ahead.

"I think this is it!" Kathryn said, pointing

to a metal door with a plaque that read "Door

100."

Chapter 10.

Before the door, there was a short brick passageway that was musty and cold, lit only by a few flickering overhead bulbs. Dean pushed open the creaky metal door labeled "Door 100" and stepped into the dimly lit hallway, Kathryn close behind.

"Ugh, it smells terrible in here," Kathryn said, scrunching her nose.

Dean's eyes scanned the hallway. "Stay alert. We don't know what might jump out at us."

Kathryn nodded, her hand drifting to the flashlight clipped to her belt. As they crept forward, their shoes scraped against debris scattered on the concrete floor - crushed soda cans, yellowed newspapers, shards of glass.

"Wait, look!" Kathryn darted forward and snatched up a plastic bottle filled with vitamins. She turned it over in her hands. "Vitamins?"

"Weird. Why would vitamins be down here?" Dean asked. Kathryn shrugged. "Who knows. They might come in handy." She shoved the bottle into her pocket.

Together they pressed forward into the darkness, ready for whatever adventure awaited them next.

Dean and Kathryn crept down the hallway, their flashlight beams cutting through the gloom. The air was heavy with dust that swirled in the shafts of light.

Every few steps, a distant roar echoed through the passageway. Kathryn's hand tightened on the flashlight. "Figure sounds close. We need to stay alert."

Dean nodded as his eyes searched the shadows. As they approached a rusted metal door, he held up a hand. "Wait. Let's check in here."

Kathryn tried the handle. Locked. She knelt, pulling a lockpick from her back pocket. With a few careful twists, the tumblers clicked into place.

The door creaked open. Beyond lay a small storage room, empty shelves gathering cobwebs. In the back corner was another door, this one was locked.

"Bingo," Dean said. He kept watch as Kathryn set to work on the lock.

Click! Kathryn yanked open the door, revealing a small breaker room tucked away inside the storage closet. It was bare except for a folded piece of paper on the floor.

Kathryn scooped it up, skimming the contents. "Dean, this is it! The instructions for the circuit breaker puzzle!"

Dean pumped his fist. "Yes! We're one step closer to getting out of this place."

From the hallway came the bone-chilling sound of Figure roaring once more, closer now. Kathryn quickly refolded the paper and tucked it away. "Let's go. We need to keep moving before Figure finds us."

Gripping their flashlights, they slipped back into the passageway. The hunt continued.

Kathryn and Dean crept along the hallway; ears strained for any sign of Figure. The instructions had mentioned ten hidden breaker switches scattered around the storage room area.

Kathryn swept her flashlight beam over the walls, searching for anything out of place. The light glinted off a small breaker switch tucked behind a dusty shelf. "There's one," she whispered.

They continued on, ducking into side rooms and alcoves. Each time they heard Figure's bellow echoing through the building, they would freeze, hardly daring to breathe.

After what felt like hours of searching, they had located five switches. Kathryn's nerves were frayed. She jumped at every skittering rat and groaning pipe.

"Just a few more," Dean said.

Dean spied a large red lever on the far wall beside a large metallic door. "Maybe that does something?"

Bracing themselves, Dean yanked the lever down with a grunt of effort.

As they entered the next room, his flashlight beam landed on a brown gangly creature with long arms.

Kathryn stifled a scream. The circular mouth full of teeth opened, issuing an ear-piercing shriek. Figure had found them.

Kathryn and Dean stumbled back as Figure's gangly arms shot out at them.

"Run!" Dean yelled.

They sprinted down the hallway, Figure's footsteps close behind. Up ahead,

Kathryn spotted the small room they'd
lockpicked earlier.

"There!" she shouted, making a
beeline for it.

"Home sweet home," Dean said as he
wedged the door shut behind them.

Figure's furious roars grew louder as it
tore at the door. Then came the sound of
rending metal.

Kathryn clicked on her flashlight and
swept it over the cluttered space. "We just
need to wait here until it's safe to head to the
breaker room."

After a while, the roaring faded.

Dean sank down against the wall with
a sigh. "You know, I could really go for a

cheese pizza right about now. And maybe some ice cream for dessert."

Kathryn gave a small laugh as she settled next to him. "I'm craving mom's mac and cheese. With extra cheese."

"Good call," Dean said. "We'll have to ask her to make us a huge batch when we get out of this place."

"Deal."

They sat in silence for a bit, listening for any signs of Figure. The creature's enraged roars had gone silent.

After several minutes with no activity, Dean carefully cracked the door open. "I think the coast is clear. Let's get to that breaker room before Figure comes back."

Flashlights in hand, they crept down the hallway toward the breaker room. The sooner they could get the power on and reach the elevator, the sooner they'd be enjoying Mom's mac and cheese.

Kathryn opened the door to the breaker room and swept her flashlight beam over the panels lining the walls.

"There it is," Dean said, pointing to a breaker box in the back. They hurried over and examined the setup.

Ten switches were labeled with numbers from 1 to 10. Above each switch was a small, darkened bulb.

"I guess we need to figure out which ones to flip on," Kathryn said.

124

Dean nodded and started throwing switches. The corresponding bulbs lit up, bathing sections of the room in a dim, flickering glow.

After some trial and error, they got four bulbs illuminated. Dean looked around the room.

"There," he said, pointing to a keypad on the wall. "We probably need to enter the sum of the numbers by the lit bulbs."

Kathryn quickly added them up. "It's 25," she said.

Dean punched the numbers into the keypad. With a loud clunk, the lights came on, flooding the entire breaker room.

"Yes!" Kathryn cheered, giving her brother a high five.

Dean grinned. "Now let's get out of here and-"

"Wait," Kathryn said, pulling the bottle of dusty vitamins from her pocket. "We should take some of these first."

Dean made a face. "I hate swallowing vitamins."

Dean took the bottle and examined the label. The expiration date was from decades ago. "Think they're still good?"

Kathryn shrugged. "One way to find out." She grabbed the bottle back, twisted off the cap, and tapped a vitamin into her palm.

Before Dean could object, she popped it into her mouth and made a face.

"Yuck, tastes like dirt."

Dean laughed. "Nice going. You sure you won't grow an extra arm or something now?"

Kathryn rolled her eyes and handed him a vitamin. "Extra arms could come in handy."

Dean blew dust off the vitamin and popped it in his mouth. "Hm, I feel nothing."

Then all of a sudden, they felt their legs tingle with newfound strength. "Wow!" Kathryn said as she felt her legs move with supernatural speed. "Let's catch that elevator!"

Dean and Kathryn burst out of the breaker room, racing up the stairwell as fast as their vitamin-charged legs could carry them. The sound of Figure's thunderous footsteps echoed up from below, getting closer by the second.

"Faster!" Kathryn yelled. She glanced over her shoulder and saw a glimpse of Figure's gangly arm reaching around the corner. His fingers scraped along the concrete wall with an awful screech.

Dean's heart pounded. He pumped his arms and willed his jelly-like legs to keep climbing.

Finally, they reached the top landing. Just a bit further and they'd be at the elevator room.

Suddenly, one of Figure's fingers shot through the gap in the stairs and grabbed Kathryn's ankle. She screamed and kicked at the scaly hand.

"Let go of her!" Dean shouted. He stomped on the creature's wrist. With a shriek, Figure released his grip.

"Come on!" Dean helped Kathryn to her feet and they sprinted the last few steps to the elevator room.

Slamming the metal cage door shut behind them, they collapsed against the cold steel bars, chests heaving. Dean reached up and hit the button. The elevator hummed to life. Figure howled in rage outside, pounding against the entrance.

"That was way too close," Kathryn said. "But we made it!"

Dean wiped sweat from his brow, listening to the creature's frustrated snarls fade into the distance. "Yeah," he said. "We're safe… I think."

The elevator jolted and began to descend with a metallic groan. Dean and Kathryn leaned against the vibrating cage walls, grateful for the break after their harrowing escape.

"I can't believe we actually did it," Kathryn said. "We made it through that nightmare maze of doors and beat all of Figure's traps."

"Yeah, no kidding." Dean glanced up nervously at the ceiling. Through the metal mesh, he could see the dark shape of Figure perched atop the elevator, peering down at them.

Kathryn followed his gaze. "Oh no, he's still chasing us! That thing just won't quit!"

"As long as we stay in here, we're safe." Dean tried to sound confident despite the uneasy flutter in his stomach.

Figure let out an ear-piercing shriek and smashed his fists against the top of the elevator. The whole thing shook violently.

"It's okay, it's okay!" he said quickly.

But his heart beat thundered in his ears.

Suddenly, a viscous drop of drool

dripped through the mesh ceiling and

splattered right onto Dean's shoulder.

"Oh gross!" he cried, wiping frantically

at the sticky goo on his sweater. "This is my

favorite sweater!"

Kathryn couldn't help but laugh at the

disgusted look on his face. "Really? That's

what you're worried about right now?"

Dean grumbled, scrubbing at the stain.

"I can't believe that freak got drool on my

clothes. Disgusting!"

Kathryn just smiled and shook her

head.

Kathryn's smile faded as she peered up the elevator shaft. There, looking down at them from above, was Ben. His eyes were full of sorrow as he watched them descend to safety without him.

"Ben..." Kathryn whispered.

But Ben's form flickered and faded as he ran away. There in his place stood the hulking shape of Figure as it clung to the top of the elevator. Its snarls echoed down the shaft.

Kathryn lowered her head. They'd made it out, but not everyone had been so lucky.

Suddenly, a bright glow began emanating from below. Dean and Kathryn shielded their eyes as the light intensified, surrounding them completely.

"What's happening?" Dean asked.

Kathryn peered into the light, her eyes widening. "It's Guiding Light!"

The benevolent entity's voice echoed around them. "You have overcome the darkness. Your will is strong and your hearts are true. Go now and be free."

As the elevator doors opened, the glow receded. Dean and Kathryn stepped out into the light of their playroom. They'd made it. They were free.

Dean grinned and asked, "Want to play again?"

"Let's play *Adopt Me* or *Brookhaven* instead," she said.

THE END

Made in the USA
Coppell, TX
24 November 2023

24640155R10075